NOW AND THEN

More views of Sutton old and new

Compiled by Frank Burgess

Design: Shirley Edwards

London Borough of Sutton Libraries and Arts Services

FOREWORD

Distance, they say, lends enchantment to the view. How much greater the enchantment, and the pleasure, when views are presented with the dexterity of mind and depth of historical perception that his many friends and admirers have come to expect from Frank Burgess.

Frank, whose home and delight Sutton and Cheam have been for close on half a century, has, I suspect, far more purpose in his hobby of recording pictorially the continuously changing backdrop to our daily lives than the mere presentation of the comparative photograph, in which technique he has specialised so successfully. He expects us to find as much of value and interest in his modern photographs as in the — sometimes century old — early comparison; we should see in them the awful warning of the need for vigilance to ensure continuing improvement in our environment, with no backsliding.

It was in recognition of his contribution in this arena that the Sutton and Cheam Society invited him in 1975 to accept the Manor of Sutton Award, which was established in 1963 to honour such contributors.

This, Mr Burgess's third publication at the hands of the London Borough of Sutton Libraries and Arts Services — to whose policy of encouraging research into, and the study of, local history due tribute must be paid — contains a further sample from his vast collection of local photographs, and illustrates, with clarity, the development of areas of Sutton neighbouring on its High Street. It demonstrates all too clearly the increase in the tempo of life, the clutter of public and private notices which assault our eyes, contrasted with the remarkable extent to which — despite the loss of many trees — Sutton is still a 'green and pleasant land'!

Thank you, Frank.

HOWARD BARRETT O.B.E.
Chairman, Friends of Whitehall, Cheam
Member, Executive Committee,
The Sutton and Cheam Society

August, 1985

First published 1985

London Borough of Sutton Libraries and Arts Services
Central Library, St. Nicholas Way, Sutton, Surrey SM1 1EA
Telephone: 01-661 5050

ISBN 0 907335 13 6

Printed and bound in Great Britain by Anchor Brendon Ltd, Tiptree, Essex

INTRODUCTION

My previous book of photographs of Sutton, *No Small Change: A hundred years of Sutton High Street,* published in 1983, seems to have aroused so much interest that I have been requested by many people to assemble another collection of old photographs, this time of points of interest beyond the High Street.

This booklet is the result: a selection from the vast collection now available to us. My main problem, indeed, was making the selection. I hope my choice has included something which will interest everyone, from old Sutton residents who may be reminded of their childhood, to new and younger residents interested in the past of our town.

In putting the photographs together, the object has been to match the old scene as closely as possible with a modern view, which has been possible in almost all cases. The accompanying notes are not an attempt to write a history of the town, but are jottings based on close analysis of the photographs and on comments from persons who have lived in the town for many more years than I have. It might in fact be thought that, in some cases, they are unnecessary as the pairs of photographs speak for themselves.

ACKNOWLEDGEMENTS

As in the case of my previous booklets, *Old Cheam* and *No Small Change,* the old photographs are reproduced from the large collection which has been gathered together with the generous help of the many owners of original photographs, postcards and other old prints. Those in the Sutton Libraries' collection are used with the permission of the Borough Librarian, Roy Smith, for which I am most grateful. They were made available to me by the willing and helpful co-operation of June Broughton, Local Studies Librarian, without whose help I could not have carried out the work.

These are friends and colleagues who are still with us, but I am sure they would agree with me that we are all indebted to the people of the past: firstly the old photographers who took and printed such superb examples of their art; then the owners who have preserved them over the years; and finally the present owners who have made them available to us. To all of these I acknowledge with gratitude my indebtedness. In addition, I apologise to anyone whose picture I may have used without their specific permission.

I would also like to express my gratitude to the designer, Shirley Edwards, another friend and member of the Libraries' staff, for the pleasing presentation of this book.

Finally, I would like to record my appreciation that my friend Howard Barrett, who devotes so much of his time to local conservation, consented to write a foreword.

My sincere thanks to them all.

F.B.
Millhall, Cheam
1985

The General Post Office in Grove Road in 1928 (on the right) and the newly built telephone exchange next door. This photograph shows that the avenue of trees in Grove Road used to extend as far as the High Street.

The modern photograph shows the fourth and fifth floor extension on the telephone exchange, and the modern Post Office built in 1952. How many people remember that, whilst the rebuilding took place, the temporary Post Office was in the building on the corner of Grove Road and Sutton Park Road?

The north side of Grove Road, again showing the trees extending to the High Street, although the modern shops have already been built.

Now that the trees have gone one can see more clearly that the shops were built in front of the old Grove Road houses, which still exist.

Grove Road as it passes Bridge Road on the left and Sutton Park Road on the right, taken in 1891. The luxuriance of the trees, stretching into the distance on both sides, makes it clear why Grove Road was so named.

It is interesting to note that, as one looks along the road, the perspective of the trees is similar to that in the old photograph. A major difference is the plethora of road markings and signs now needed to control the traffic flow.

12 Grove Road, Sutton.

Another view of Grove Road, looking towards the High Street, when the avenue of trees was complete. The road on the left is the top of Sutton Park Road and the houses are those that still exist behind the modern shop premises in the photograph opposite.

Sutton Park Road at the turn of the century, when it was a quiet residential road. Note the great number of horse-chestnut trees. In the 1950s the Highways Committee adopted a recommendation of the Parks Superintendent that half of them should be taken out to allow the remainder to grow to maturity.

The trees are now over a hundred years old, and although one by one they are succumbing to disease, there is still a goodly avenue. This once quiet residential road, however, is now part of the busy one-way traffic circuit.

Cheam Road in 1903, looking from the top of Robin Hood Lane towards the High Street.

These two pictures largely speak for themselves, but it might be noted that the burr brick wall containing the raised verge has survived, albeit rather knocked about and neglected.

An earlier view of Cheam Road, taken in 1890, a little nearer the High Street, in which trees predominate more than ever.

This is an example of how present-day street 'furniture', i.e. the lamp column, spoils the view, if one uses the precise camera position used for the old photograph.

Like the cover pictures, this pair shows a dramatic change in St. Nicholas Way since 1900. They are taken from Cheam Road looking into St. Nicholas Road, now St. Nicholas Way, with the kerb and fence line on the right-hand side common to both; likewise the spire of St. Nicholas Church.

Between the Civic Offices and the College of Liberal Arts, but not visible in the picture, is the Central Library, in whose local collection many of the old photographs used in this book may be found.

There is not quite such a great time gap between these two views of the entrance to Cheam Road from the High Street. The older picture was taken in 1932, four years before the traffic signals were installed.

The buildings are substantially the same. The interest here is in the street scene: the vehicles, the street lighting, and the people themselves and how their dress has changed.

Cheam Road again, in about 1912, looking westwards with the High School for Boys on the left and Sutton Picture Theatre on the right. Patrons would alight from their carriages and proceed up wide steps through the raised verge.

Alas, most of the trees have gone and the old cinema, subsequently the Curzon, has not only changed its name but also its face.

A better view of the Cheam Road Picture Theatre in 1928. This cinema was one of the earliest (but not the first) in the town, built in 1911.

Although the appearance of the front is now so different, and the inside has been altered, the main structure remains intact behind the new façade.

The Plaza Cinema, Carshalton Road, one of Sutton's modern cinemas, built in 1934 and demolished in 1979. In its later years it was renamed the Granada and has now been replaced by the modern office block, 'Sutton Park House'.

Across the road from the cinema stood the Congregational Church, built in 1889 and demolished in 1975. A little further along the road towards Carshalton stood the Wesleyan Chapel, built in 1884 and vacated in 1907 when their new church was opened in Cheam Road. It then became Sutton Hippodrome, an early 'electric theatre', after which it was used as an engineering works.

Carshalton Road.   Sutton.

Memory is often unreliable, and this pair of photographs, proving where the two churches shown on the previous page actually stood, may surprise many people.

Manor Park House, the former Central Library (with a library extension built on at the left) was demolished in 1976. The house was previously a boys' private school, and one of the ancillary buildings still survives, just visible on the right in both photographs.

Sutton Manor. These are the sole surviving illustrations of the Manor House, which stood in extensive grounds on the north side of Manor Lane.

Manor Park formed no part of the Manor estate. The estate was sold in 1896, and the land developed with properties in Lodge Road (now obliterated by Throwley Way), Lenham Road, Litchfield Road and the northern length of Warwick Road.

50283. Sutton, County School & Fire Station. FF & Co.

Throwley Road looking towards the High Street, with the old County School (later the Art School) on the right of the picture, and the Fire Station, with the Municipal Offices beyond. The top of the tower visible above is that of the Baptist Church which stood on the corner of High Street and Hill Road.

All the buildings in the old view have now gone and the once quiet road now carries all the 'up-town' traffic until the whole southern circuit is completed.

Throwley Road Baths, built in 1903, contained slipper baths for men and women as well as the swimming bath. Many Sutton children learned to swim here and this photograph must bring back many memories.

The scene has changed but the street trees remain. Although not planted when the old photograph was taken, a pair of yew trees flanked the entrance to the Baths in later years. One of the pair still survives.

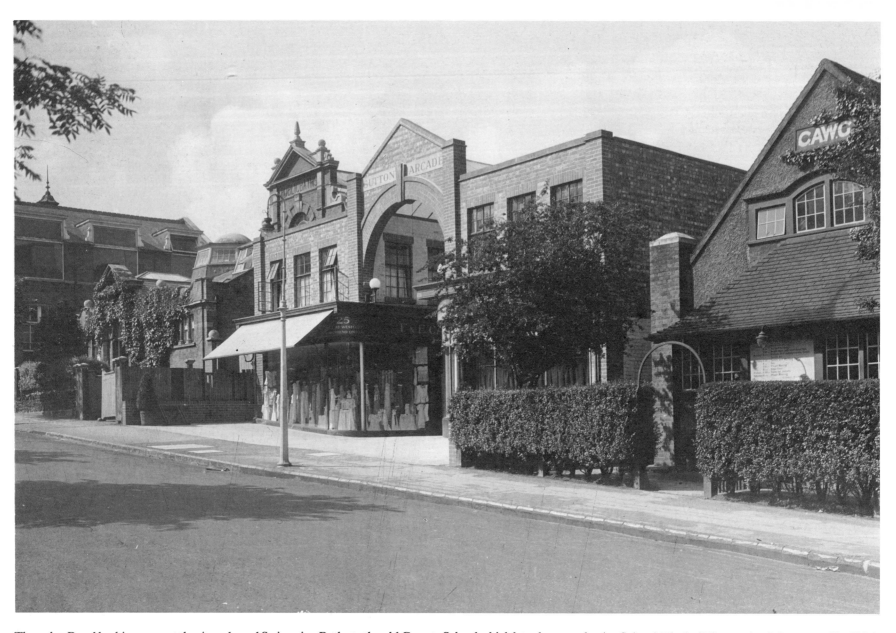

Throwley Road looking up past the Arcade and Swimming Baths to the old County School which later became the Art School. The building on the right, erected in 1906, was later occupied by the Christian Alliance of Women and Girls, later to become the YWCA. The site was later occupied by the goods entrance of Woolworth's old shop.

Now only the Sutton Arcade remains, with Surrey House occupying the site of both the Baths and the Art School.

The Skating Rink in Throwley Road, remembered better as the Gliderdrome. It started life in 1909 with steel-wheeled skates, which must have been terribly noisy; it was later converted to a Billiards Hall and reconverted for use with rubber-wheeled skates in 1936. It was claimed to be the biggest roller skating floor in England; and was demolished in the late 1960s.

There are no clues in the modern photograph to help locate the site of the Gliderdrome, but from memory and research on old maps, I can say with confidence that the kerb line in this matching photograph is the same as in the old picture.

PRINTERS.

Lind Road, Sutton.

S&W. Series. 986.

Lind Road, looking north, at the southern end of which is the Jenny Lind public house, was the main spine road of Sutton New Town, built during Queen Victoria's reign and consisting almost entirely of small residences.

Although the present view looks much the same, with the exception of all the cars, more than half the premises are now in industrial or commercial use.

This old photograph was taken from Vernon Road in 1870 and shows, in the distance, the original Windsor Castle public house standing in Lind Road, on what became Sutton District Water Company land.

In the present-day view, almost all that is missing is the Windsor Castle.

When the Sutton District Water Company cleared the land for their works, the public house was replaced by this one of the same name in Greyhound Road.

The dear old Public Hall in 1900, scene of so many interesting and enjoyable functions, built as a private venture in 1878. It was acquired by Sutton Urban District Council in 1920, and eventually demolished in 1981.

In its early days it was the home of the fire brigade. The fire escape was kept in the shed as shown, but the steam pump was housed beneath the stage, reached through a door in the side of the building.

Air conditioned
OFFICE BUILDING
56 000 square feet
TO BE LET
Hillier Parker
01·629 7666

HILL ROAD

The modern office building erected on the site of the Public Hall in 1984.

The Cottage Hospital in Hill Road photographed in 1902 soon after completion. This building superseded a small one in Bushey Road, and was itself superseded in 1931 by the present hospital in Chiltern Road.

When the hospital was demolished, the site was developed. A substantial shop, with flats above, was erected, which traded as Surrey Home Stores, a general grocer's, for many years.

The Baptist Church in Hill Road in 1891. The small building in the centre of the picture was erected first as their Chapel, and the main church built in 1884.

In 1934 Mr Shinner bought the site and with the proceeds the Baptists built their fine modern church in Cheam Road. Mr Shinner extended his store from the High Street round the corner into Hill Road, as shown here and on the following pages.

Before he acquired the church, Mr Shinner had clad his range of old shops with the modern style faience-clad façade.

He then demolished the church and built on the site a completely new building to match his lower shop. The fact that all the old buildings and the new one are on a steep hill explains the somewhat inconvenient differences in floor levels within the store.

Crocus Cottage and Snowdrop Cottage on the bend in St. Nicholas Road alongside the churchyard, where Lucy Green's cottage school used to stand. They were demolished in 1960 when St. Nicholas House was built.

St. Nicholas House was aligned to allow for the eventual construction of St. Nicholas Way.

Old cottages in St. Nicholas Road, near the corner of High Street. When they were demolished, an early motor garage was built by Howard Smallman Garages. The business later became Surrey Motors, who named the premises Speedway House.

On the right of both pictures the High Street can be seen, on the corner of which Messrs. Burton's modern building certainly changes the view.

ST. Nicholas Road, Sutton.   45. P.   S&W. Series.

St. Nicholas Road in about 1915, with the garage later to become Surrey Motors' Speedway House on the right, opposite a row of cottages which stood at the rear of Amos Reynolds' High Street shop.

Speedway House was demolished in 1960 to enable St. Nicholas House, above, to be built, but Surrey Motors retained a showroom and a petrol forecourt until 1979, where Bejam's now stands.

Robin Hood Lane, Sutton

It is not uncommon for there to be old footpaths or bridleways from one parish to another. The one from St. Nicholas Church to St. Dunstan's Church crossed Robin Hood Lane at this point, where the path from the churchyard crosses into Camden Road.

The present street scene is interesting in comparison: with fewer trees and the inevitable traffic and road markings; but a wire pedestrian barrier is in the same place as the posts and rail, and the sewer vent column still exists.

The Robin Hood public house, photographed in 1870 when it was decorated with mock half-timber work, as were the cottages at the rear. The ornateness of the decoration contrasts sharply with its appearance today.

Diver's Ditch, the pond in West Street which was on the spring line between Epsom and Croydon. This photograph is believed to have been taken by Lewis Hind in about 1865.

The pond was filled up, according to local historian C. J. Marshall, in 1866, and houses were built on the firm ground behind it in 1869. These were demolished in 1982 and the temporary car park constructed.

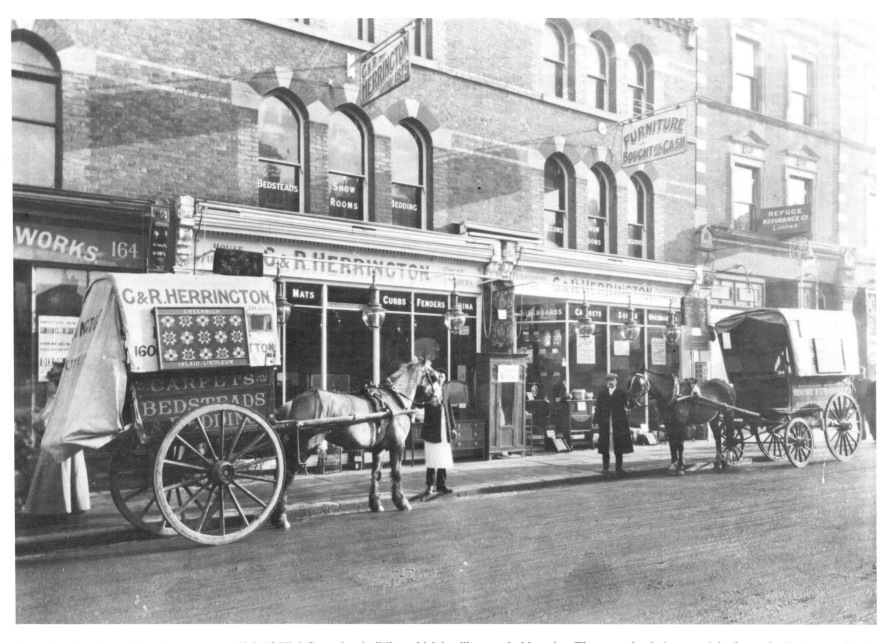

G. and R. Herrington's furniture store at 160/162 High Street in a building which is still recognisable today. The two-wheeled cart and the four-wheeled wagon for the delivery of furniture are very different from modern motor pantechnicons.

Who would ever have imagined, three-quarters of a century ago, that the High Street could ever be closed to wheeled traffic, and have a public toilet installed in front of the shops!

One of Francis Frith's fine photographs, showing Sutton Green in 1903, with the London Road leading up to the Angel cutting with the pedestrian bridge across it.

This land, bounded by the row of elm trees, was originally part of Sutton Common, and in the enclosure award of 1809 it was granted to the townspeople as a public open space.

This 1985 photograph is notable for the absence of elm trees, although trees and shrubs are still prolific. Amongst them, hidden discreetly, is a public convenience, now disused and replaced by the very public 'superloo' shown in the previous page.

The trolley-bus turn-around at the Green. The electric trams from Croydon, which the trolleys replaced in 1935, could not negotiate the sharp corner at the Grapes, but could shunt on to the return track; whereas the trolley buses needed to turn. As they could take the right-angled corner at Benhill Avenue, they proceeded as far as Bushey Road where they could turn around. The trolley buses ceased to operate in 1961.

Victoria Pond at Sutton Green, opposite "The Cricketers" inn. An early photograh shows the pond as a rather dirty discharge point for surface water drains, but by the time of Queen Victoria's coronation it was an ornamental feature with an island, on which was planted a 'Coronation' tree.

During the last war the pond was designated as an emergency water suply for fire fighting, but by 1955 the pond was drained, filled up and laid out as a small enclosed garden.

Angel Bridge, one of the landmarks of old Sutton, photographed by Frith in 1932. Although the bus approaching is a covered double-decker, the open-topped type was still about; consequently the legend on the bridge was very important: "Low Bridge: bus passengers remain seated"!

What a difference modern design makes to our environment. Apart from the change in appearance, the raising of the bridge to modern clearance requirements necessitated more steps, which are now so steep as to be difficult for the aged and infirm and quite impossible for the disabled.

Two views from the Angel Bridge taken in 1932 and 1985. Whilst the loss of the trees is to be deplored, it has at least extended the view to the higher part of the town with the modern tower blocks showing on the skyline.

38924. SUTTON COMMON ROAD. F.F.&Cº

Sutton Common road in 1896. This literally was the road across the common, which was enclosed in 1809. By the time the photograph was taken, the land had been developed with substantial houses in extensive grounds, occupied, in many cases, by the town's successful businessmen.

After the last war, it was impossible to obtain staff for the big houses with their extensive gardens. At the same time, housing was in great demand; and these two facts resulted in the big houses being demolished and new housing estates taking their place. In many cases, the new roads took the old house names as in Fairlands Avenue and Hurstcourt Road off Sutton Common Road.

The Bandstand which stood in Manor Park, just about where the infants' play enclosure is today. It became unsafe shortly after the war and was demolished in the 1950s.